Join our gentle protest for presence and receive news and offers for forthcoming inner work projects:

www.innerworkproject.com

D1513362

Each Inner Workbook is a self-study retreat or workshop that you can do at home. They are designed to become a part of your day, just like that first cup of tea, and invite you to journal the experience as you develop your practice, making it your own.

See What Happens

Contents

Introduction:
What are affirmations?
04

Affirmations
& inner work
08

How to create
affirmations
10

The journal
of affirmations
16

Introduction:
What are affirmations?

Positive affirmations are personal statements made in the present tense, encouraging us to live as we wish to live right here, right now, not in a hazy distant future that may or may not happen.

The simplest and often most effective affirmations begin with, 'I am', followed by a positive assertion. Affirmations can also be visual – for example, putting together a collage of images that illustrate your inner desires. They are present in your energy; for instance, you might affirm your openness to new ideas as you walk into a meeting with colleagues.

Affirmations offer an opportunity to get up close and personal with ourselves, with the gifts we have to bring to the world, and with our gratitude. Affirmations bring us back in touch with what and who inspires us; they invite magic and joy into our day, strengthen our resolve or determination, and sharpen our focus on what matters.

Affirmations can help us reframe what we feel we are worthy of and release old limiting stories we may believe about ourselves. They ask us to choose how we want to live, express our desires and have the courage to follow our inner compass.

Affirmations open us up to a natural state of abundance and expansiveness, encouraging a flow of giving and receiving.

Affirmations use the power of words to bring thoughts into reality, giving them a vibration. You can repeat affirmations aloud or silently say them in your mind's eye. You might find looking into the mirror a powerful way to express your affirmations or you may wish to whisper them to nature.

Writing affirmations down, journaling, drawing, finding quotes or lines of poetry all nourish the energy of your affirmations and are creative ways of finding out about yourself. Writing things down has also been shown to help strengthen the intention and belief behind our thoughts, bringing them to life.

Affirmation
inspiration
Here are
some examples:

I am inspired by things happening all around me.
I am grateful for the people I have in my life.
I grow every day.
I treat myself kindly and with compassion.
I am able to learn from all situations.
I am grateful for the things I have in life.
I appreciate the opportunities I am given.
I am kind and help inspire others to be kind.
My life is full of potential.
I give myself permission to be myself.
I give myself permission to take time for myself.
I have the power to change.
I forgive those who have hurt me.
I have the ability to recover from difficulties.
I am courageous.
I am capable of standing up for myself.
I love myself fully.
I am good at _____.
I have value.

I am at peace with who I am.
I deserve peace and joy in my life.
I am worthy of love.
I have many positive qualities, including _____.
I surround myself with positive, supportive people.
I am enough.
My needs and desires are important.
I am worthy of respect and kindness.
I choose to celebrate my good qualities.
I am good enough.
I am empowered to take my own path.
I put my energy into the things that matter to me.
I am free to create the life I desire.
I am capable of making my own decisions.
I trust in my ability to make good decisions.
I deserve success.
I give myself permission to do what is right for me.
I give myself the time and space to grow and learn.
I have the freedom to set my own goals.
I am open to future opportunities.
I am in charge of my life.
I can control how I react to others.
My emotions have purpose and value.
I trust myself.
I accept myself just the way I am.
I feel safe.
I am calm.
I am peace.
I have the power to let things go.

Affirmations & inner work

Affirmations are a gateway for doing inner work as they offer an opportunity to explore the universal question, Who Am I? This allows for curiosity, which is one of the best pathways to inner growth, understanding and expansion.

When created and expressed with self-compassion, affirmations can help us with the inner healing process. They invite us to love all parts of ourselves, to nourish ourselves and give ourselves the credit we deserve and the love we are worthy of.

Affirmations help you to get closer to what you really want because if you're willing to be honest with yourself, then you will know which are meaningful to you. Your heart will tell you, 'Yes, this one'. You might have to listen out for it to start with; go beneath the protestations of your inner critic who is more used to being heard. Like most things that are worth doing, it takes a bit of practice.

Affirmations are an essential part of the manifesting process, because as you practise and identify those that are truly in alignment with your inner self, then somehow life gets into the flow at the same time.

Over time, positive affirmations can help you make long-lasting changes to the ways you think and feel, actually forging new pathways in the brain and allowing old ones to lessen their grip. Human beings tend towards having a negativity bias, which means that you might be more likely to hold on to negative beliefs you have about yourself than positive ones, or think that if you are ready to cope with the worst-case scenario you can imagine for any given situation, then you will be prepared for anything. But the problem with this approach, is that you not only devote a great deal of precious energy to imagining what could go wrong, but you might also miss positive experiences that are right in front of you.

Practising daily affirmations
for a month will shine a light on
your inner dreams and the gifts
you have to offer. Bringing these
out into the open can make you
feel vulnerable and the process
takes courage. Be playful with
them, and imagine you are your
own best friend. Where your
attention goes, energy flows.

We Are Awake

How to:
Create affirmations

When we give ourselves a few minutes at the start of the day to breathe, look within and connect with what we appreciate in our lives, we are practising the power of presence, so that even as challenges arise during the day, we might stay in the moment and respond rather than react. We are attentive to our lives.

We are awake.

People who meditate in the morning are more likely to report having a good day than those who don't. It's also the best time of the day to set your intention – where is your focus going to be today? You don't need to spend hours on your morning routine to feel the benefits – just a few minutes, even over a cup of tea, giving a little thanks, inviting a little magic into your day, deciding on what matters.

You may prefer to be spontaneous with your affirmations and simply prompt yourself each morning with the words, 'I am...', and see what comes. Or you might want to focus on developing an attitude of abundance and so choose a few specific affirmations that resonate with you.

This workbook is divided into four weeks that are designed to take you on a journey with affirmations, encouraging daily practice. Week 1 is for tuning into the potential of affirmations through gratitude, love and appreciation; week 2 is for aligning with your inner compass; week 3 acknowledges any resistance with compassion and curiosity; and week 4 celebrates ways to put your affirmations (and therefore your gifts) out into the Universe.

Why keep an affirmation journal?

By taking the time to reflect on your affirmations, you begin to build a map of your practice. This helps you to learn from your experiences instead of repeating the same patterns over and over.

Keeping a journal is a way of processing information, helping to bring clarity to your experiences. Writing is also a way to process stress, emotions and trauma. If difficulties come up around a particular affirmation, for example, writing about them and how you feel can offer some release.

Over time, this kind of journal provides a rich history of your inner life. It is a way to practise deepening your self-expression and marking moments of discovery, understanding or great confusion (often the most interesting, if frustrating, times on the journey).

A practice:
Morning affirmation

Sit or stand in front of a mirror, relaxed but with your back straight. Breathe naturally, and begin to just observe the breath and the rhythm of the inhale...

followed by the exhale...

Allow your shoulders to drop, letting go of any tension.

"Good morning."

Check in with how you are feeling, take as long as you need.

What would it be good for you to hear today?

Consider:

Today, I am grateful for...
Today, I am...

If you would like to choose from the following, go ahead, or feel free to create your own at any time:

I trust
I invite
I see
I love
I am worthy of
I choose
I give
I receive
I release
I let go of
I accept
I belong to
I was made for

Feel into it and sense when your inner energy is aligned with the words you choose, when your emotions connect and you feel a spark, a warm feeling or a little 'Aha, yes'.

Visualize each affirmation as a healing light or energy. Give it a colour and warmth and allow it to flow into you, up through the soles of your feet or down through the crown of your head, or it might wish to form a lovely bubble of energy around you. Whatever feels right for you.

Write your affirmations down in your journal and then imagine them floating free into the day, bouncing around the Universe in a lovely bubble of energy and giving out and attracting good vibes wherever they go.

See What Happens

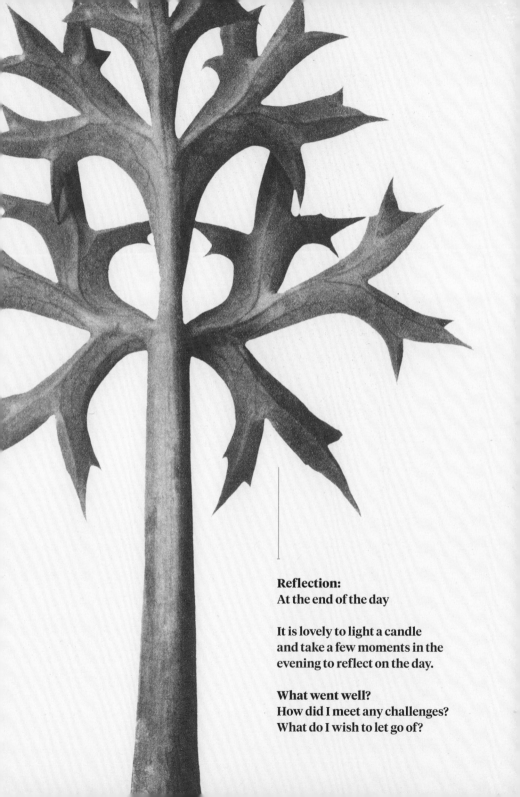

Reflection:
At the end of the day

It is lovely to light a candle
and take a few moments in the
evening to reflect on the day.

What went well?
How did I meet any challenges?
What do I wish to let go of?

A simple mantra is
om shanti shanti shanti

Shanti means 'peace' in Pali, an
Indian language, and this mantra
can help centre, focus and bring
peace to your mind, body
and spirit.

See what happens

Take this month to explore different affirmations – to try them on for size and see what feels good in the moment. Don't be too quick to edit your choices. Have fun, play with them, put them into songs. You might be drawn to certain affirmations and then feel you should dismiss them because they are too much or you're not really worthy of them. This is the time to reframe what you feel you are worthy of.

Crystals for affirmations

1. **Rose quartz**
   for love and gratitude
2. **Citrine**
   for affirmations of abundance
3. **Sodalite**
   for knowing what you really want
4. **Selenite**
   for clarity and self-awareness

Essential oils for affirmations

1. **Peppermint**
   for clarity
2. **Bergamot**
   for self-acceptance
3. **Eucalyptus**
   for wellness
4. **Cedarwood**
   for focus

Mantras & affirmations

A mantra is not the same as an affirmation, but can help to calm the mind and bring you into a more meditative, expansive state. Ready for your affirmations.

A mantra is an ancient sacred sound, word or phrase with a particular vibration that when repeated is designed to help bring you into alignment with the Universe. Mantras are used in both the Hindu and Buddhist traditions, but tend to be used more for meditation in the Buddhist tradition. You can repeat the sound as a chant either aloud or silently as even when repeated silently, it will vibrate within you. 'Mantra' is Sanskrit and is often translated to mean 'liberation of the mind'. You might wish to use a mantra to help you tune in, making it a little easier to create affirmations that are in true alignment with your essence or your heart.

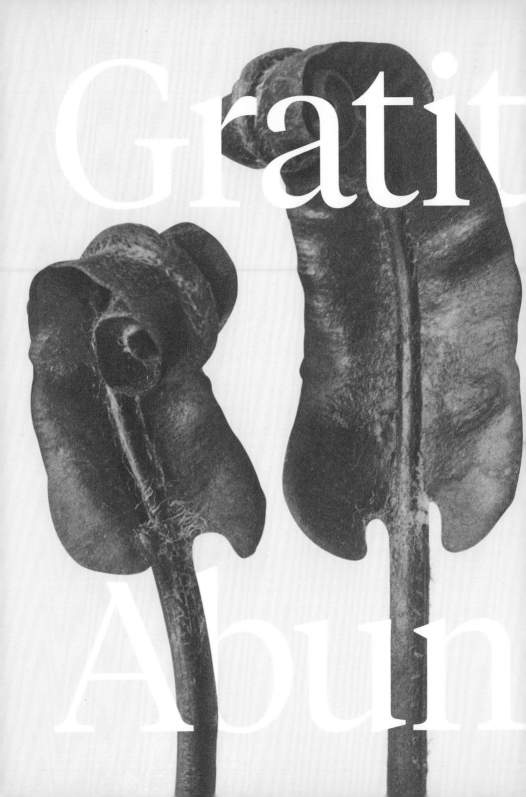

Gratit

Abun

Habits are human nature. Why not create some that will mint gold?

Hafiz

Week 1:
Gratitude
& abundance

Day 1

A meditation:
Appreciation for what is

Find a comfortable place to sit, relaxed but with your back straight. Drop your shoulders and relax into the natural rhythm of your breath. You can either read the meditation through and then close your eyes or you can use the words as a gentle guide once you have settled.

As you settle and quietly observe your breath, you begin to feel a deep appreciation for this breath that gives you life. You can appreciate your miraculous body which does so much for you, nourished by the breath. Take a moment to thank your body, to thank your incredible imagination, your generous heart. You may wish to thank the air for giving so much life, as well as the water and the earth. And then, begin to consider those closest to you in your life, and how you appreciate all that they give to you and all that you give to them. Think about those a little further out: colleagues, neighbours or the people you meet and just say hello to while out and about.

I am grateful

You appreciate all the moments of connection, nurture and nourishment these bring you. You begin to appreciate your wider community that does its best to help those in need. You appreciate all the sentient beings in your environment, from the friendly dogs to the pollinating bees that mean the crops can grow the vital food you are so grateful for. You appreciate all the incredible ecosystems of the world, of which you are a part. The networks of rivers, the awe-inspiring mountains, the rich soil, the forests that breathe out oxygen into the air for you to breathe in. You appreciate all the beauty and the generosity of the Earth that nourishes you. And as you come back to the breath, feel how far and wide the energy of your appreciation has expanded in these moments. And you come back into your body, feel the seat beneath you, you wiggle your fingers and toes, and when you're ready, you're ready...

Date:

Evening Reflection

Today, I am grateful for:

What went well?

What would it be good for me to hear today?

How did I meet any challenges?

Today, I am:

What do I wish to let go of?

Week 1:
Gratitude
& abundance

Day 2
Inspired by

Whether it's Rumi's poetry or your best friend who blows your mind daily with her courage, inspiration is deep nourishment for our affirmations. Jot down a few notes here on what and who inspires you and why. And what do others find inspiring about you?

Write down inspiring ideas, scenes, moments, quotes, write poetry!

I am
inspired

See What Happens

Date:

Who inspires me?

What is inspiring about me?

Why?

Why?

Week 1:
Gratitude & abundance

Day 3
Nourished by

Draw yourself in the centre of the page opposite (a stick person is fine). Now surround yourself with all the things and beings you can think of that nourish you in some way. Give yourself a few minutes to jot these down around you or feel free to draw them. Come back to this page when you think of something else you can add.

My body needs it –
the hot baths, the care,
the soft water, the
perfume, the warmth.
I take on the colours of
the flowers, the bloom,
the delicacy. It
becomes me.

Anaïs Nin

I am nourished

Date:

Me

Week 1:
Gratitude & abundance

Day 4
Feeling abundant

It's a lovely, generous, expansive feeling to sense the abundance of the Universe, that it is good to have deep desires, to give and receive and allow abundance to flow. Shakti Gawain calls this 'realizing our natural state of prosperity and plenty on all levels'. She acknowledges that there is a reality of poverty and starvation for many people in the world at this time, 'but we do not need to keep creating and perpetuating that reality'. The key is to open ourselves to the possibility that there is enough to go around, if we change our ways to be 'balanced and harmonious with one another and with the Earth that nourishes us'.

To live in a state of abundance is to live in alignment with our values, to be able to offer our unique gifts to the world in the ways that we can, to immerse ourselves in the rich detail of the present moment, whether this is a delicious taste, an invigorating blast of sea air or a touch that came just as it was needed. To be on this unique, life-giving, beautiful planet.

When happiness is shared, it grows. Your happiness contributes to the collective, you doing what you really love contributes so much. You feel rewarded and appreciated for your efforts, knowing within that you are enough and that abundance is your natural state of being.

I embrace the natural flow of abundance

See What Happens

Date:

Evening Reflection

Today, I am grateful for:

What went well?

What would it be good
for me to hear today?

How did I meet any challenges?

Today, I am:

What do I wish to let go of?

Week 1:
Gratitude
& abundance

Day 5
Awe & wonder

In turns out that awe, wonder and amazement are good for our health and our sense of happiness, even our clarity of thinking. We perform well on awe and wonder, and far less so on self-criticism or shame. Apparently, awe even makes us kinder and more generous – who knew?

Cultivate awe in everyday life by inviting it in.

I invite wonder to cross my path today

66

Awe shifts our attention away from our small sense of self and opens us to feeling that we are part of something greater. Awe inspires self-transcendence.

Shauna Shapiro,
Good Morning, I Love You

See What Happens

Date:

Evening Reflection

Today, I am grateful for:

What went well?

What would it be good for me to hear today?

How did I meet any challenges?

Today, I am:

What do I wish to let go of?

Week 1:
Gratitude
& abundance

Day 6
Clear the clutter

It's a simple idea but it really does work. As you clear your physical clutter you create space for your inner world at the same time. You begin to question what you need or don't need, what others would benefit from you giving away, and what's important. Perhaps there is a room in your home where you can even create a space that is sacred to you, whether that's with a beautiful, cosy cushion or blanket, or where you keep your crystals and oracle cards. Where you can sit for a few minutes in the morning to set your intentions and state your affirmations for the day. Where you can just be... and breathe...

I feel light & uninhibited

Think of your house as an allegory for your body. Keep cleaning it every day.

Shoukei Matsumoto,
A Monk's Guide to a Clean House and Mind

Date:

Evening Reflection

Today, I am grateful for:

What went well?

What would it be good for me to hear today?

How did I meet any challenges?

Today, I am:

What do I wish to let go of?

Week 1:
Gratitude & abundance

Day 7
Vision board

This is a classic manifesting exercise for good reason, bringing the power of visual affirmations onto the page and into your life. You do need to do a little prep for this and gather some lovely magazines you are attracted to, some scissors, glue and a big piece of card.

Go through the magazines cutting out images and words that call to you. You might find a theme starts to develop, or that some images are more powerful than others, resonating with your inner dreams and desires.

Play around and make a collage in any way you like. Just go for it.

Stand back and admire your vision! Let it all soak in and flow out into the Universe.

I see

Date:

Evening Reflection

Today, I am grateful for:

What went well?

What would it be good for me to hear today?

How did I meet any challenges?

Today, I am:

What do I wish to let go of?

Com

Inner

> ❝
>
> Let yourself be silently drawn by the strange pull of what you really love.
>
> Rumi

pass

Week 2:
Inner compass

Day 8
Finding your inner compass

To find the part of you that knows the way, give yourself a little time each day just to check in and notice how you are. Notice the signals your body gives you: what is your gut feeling? Is your heart saying 'Yes!'? Follow those good feelings.

Practise listening to your intuition when you are making choices and start making notes of any hunches you have.

As you align your inner compass, your affirmations will come from this inner knowing, from the essence of who you are. Listen out for the whispers within.

I am listening

See What Happens

Date:

Evening Reflection

Today, I am grateful for:

What went well?

What would it be good for me to hear today?

How did I meet any challenges?

Today, I am:

What do I wish to let go of?

Week 2:
Inner compass

Day 9
Values

When your affirmations are in alignment with your values, their power is greatly amplified. Pick two values from the list below that sing out to you the most and weave them into your affirmations for today.

Adaptability	Efficiency	Independence	Resourcefulness
Adventure	Equality	Initiative	Respect
Altruism	Excellence	Integrity	Self-discipline
Ambition	Fairness	Intuition	Self-expression
Authenticity	Family	Joy	Self-respect
Balance	Freedom	Justice	Serenity
Beauty	Friendship	Kindness	Service
Belonging	Fun	Knowledge	Simplicity
Caring	Future generations	Leadership	Spirituality
Collaboration	Generosity	Learning	Stewardship
Community	Giving back	Love	Success
Compassion	Grace	Loyalty	Trust
Competence	Gratitude	Make a difference	Truth
Contribution	Growth	Openness	Understanding
Courage	Harmony	Optimism	Usefulness
Creativity	Health	Order	Vision
Curiosity	Home	Patience	Wealth
Dignity	Honesty	Peace	Well-being
Diversity	Hope	Personal fulfilment	Wholeheartedness
Environment	Inclusion	Power	Wisdom

Date:

Evening Reflection

Today, I am grateful for:

What went well?

What would it be good for me to hear today?

How did I meet any challenges?

Today, I am:

What do I wish to let go of?

Week 2:
Inner compass

Day 10
A prompt:
I love

Fill the page with
everything you love. You can
jot these down in words or
draw pictures if you wish.

Week 2:
Inner compass

Day 11
Anchoring affirmations in the body

The chakras are a system of energy centres in the body; there are seven main chakras from the root or base chakra at the base of the spine to the crown chakra at the top of the head. You can anchor your affirmations in your body at these chakra points, while at the same time allowing them to float free as good vibrations around the Universe.

Find the energy centre or chakra that feels aligned with your affirmation and imagine it surrounded by the colour of that chakra in the associative part of your body. The chakras are thought to have a spinning kind of energy, and when in balance will spin nicely at a pace that feels energizing but not out of control.

Energy flows through me

Crown
(Top of head):
I am connected
(Violet-white)

Third eye
(Between eyes):
I am clear-sighted
(Purple)

Throat
I am expressive
(Blue)

Heart
(Chest):
I am loving
(Green & pink)

Sacral
(Just below belly button):
I am experiencing
(Orange)

Solar plexus
(Stomach):
I am powerful
(Yellow)

Root
(Base of spine):
I am grounded
(Red)

See What Happens

Date:

Evening Reflection

Today, I am grateful for:

What went well?

What would it be good for me to hear today?

How did I meet any challenges?

Today, I am:

What do I wish to let go of?

Week 2:
Inner compass

Day 12
A meditation: Knowing what you want

Settle into the moment with three deep breaths, in through your nose and out through your nose. Let your energy sink into the lower half of your body on each exhale, feeling the support of the ground beneath you. Let your shoulders drop and let any tension out.

Spend a few minutes completing the statements on the opposite page. Write whatever comes to mind with no self-editing, adding as much specific detail as you can. Go deep, go far: you can say right here what you most long for, what your heart and soul desire.

Once you have written for a few minutes, read what you have noted down and then speak your truth, completing the following statement:

What I really want is

I want:

I long for:

I need:

Week 2:
Inner compass

Day 13
A practice: Walking into your future

This practice is from *Becoming Supernatural* by Dr Joe Dispenza, who writes: 'When there's a vibrational match between your energy and that future potential that already exists in the quantum field, that future event is going to find you – or better yet, your body will be drawn to a new reality. You become a magnet to a new destiny, which will manifest as an unknown, new experience.'

Or as Rumi said a couple of thousand years ago...'What you seek is seeking you '.

Imagine your future reality as if it already exists here in the present moment. Imagine your body picking up the vibration from that future reality, coming across to you like the vibration from a tuning fork. Your body is also like a tuning fork, harmonizing with the future – you're on the same frequency. 'That's the moment your future finds you. This is how you create new realities.'

When you sense that you are in tune, begin to walk as this future self and embody the future 'you' right now in your thoughts, feelings and actions. As Dr Dispenza describes, you 'get into the habit' of walking as this new reality of you, whether that's as a wealthy or healthy person, a confident person or a totally chilled-out person.

I am

I am:

Week 2:
Inner compass

Day 14
Affirming your intentions

Unlike a set goal, an intention is a guiding principle for how you want to live your life. An intention can help you focus on your purpose as a way of life, an attitude, rather than what you want to achieve.

One-word intentions can have great clarity, meaning and power. They are easy to check in with when you are faced with a challenge or dilemma – you can ask yourself, 'How does this feel in relation to my intention?'

Here are some examples of one-word intentions. Look out for yours in the world around you or in your dreams.

Truth
Wisdom
Collaboration
Creativity
Depth

Expansion
Learning
Wild
Simplicity
Healing

Today I send out the arrow of my intent

See What Happens

Date:

Evening Reflection

Today, I am grateful for:

What went well?

Words I could live by:

How did I meet any challenges?

Today, I am:

What do I wish to let go of?

ving

66

No matter how old you are, you can actually sculpt new healthy pathways in the brain and prune away old, unhealthy ones.

Shauna Shapiro, *Good Morning I Love You*

stance

Week 3:
Dissolving resistance

Day 15
A meditation: Smile yoga

Sit comfortably as you do this meditation and take your time. Relax into the natural rhythm of your breath and, as you do so, turn up the corners of your mouth into a subtle, gentle smile. This is sometimes called 'the Buddha's half smile'.

Imagine this gentle smile now gradually radiating through your entire body. Soften into it and welcome it, relaxing any tension with its openness. Give space to this inner smile. Do not cover up any worries or pain with the smile, but just allow it to be there... in your heart, your eyes, massaging your tired shoulders.

Bring to mind a dear one; they might be a person or a pet who loves and trusts you. Begin to sense this being in all their goodness, in all the ways that you love and care for them. Send them your good wishes and sense how they receive these:

May you be happy
May you be filled with love and kindness
May you accept yourself just as you are.

Now open yourself up to your own innate goodness, all the ways in which you are loved by them. Take in their love, imagine them coming close to you, look into their eyes and see this love and trust. Now send the same good wishes to yourself:

May you be happy
May you be filled with love and kindness
May you accept yourself just as you are.

Receive these wishes and step into your day.

Date:

Evening Reflection

Today, I am grateful for:

What went well?

What would it be good for me to hear today?

How did I meet any challenges?

Today, I am:

What do I wish to let go of?

Week 3:
Dissolving resistance

Day 16
Acknowledge & release

Affirmations do not serve us fully if we only acknowledge positive vibes and deny any negative thoughts or feelings. Just think, often the best thing that a good friend will do for us is to listen when we are upset, to witness and acknowledge our feelings, while as a child perhaps we were encouraged to 'be brave' or 'don't cry'.

For difficult emotions to move through and not get stuck in our minds and bodies, give them permission to be felt and acknowledged while knowing that you are not, in essence, your emotions. Sense the tension in your body, identify the emotion and accept it. Be curious about why you are feeling the emotion. Don't try to control it. **Let it be.**

I let go of what no longer serves me

> Be like a tree. Stay grounded, keep growing, and know when to let go.

TinyBuddha

Date:

Evening Reflection

Today, I am grateful for:

What went well?

What would it be good for me to hear today?

How did I meet any challenges?

Today, I am:

What do I sense it is time to let go of:

Week 3:
Dissolving resistance

Day 17
Curiosity

When an affirmation becomes a question

I am safe.

Am I really?
What does that mean exactly?

Stay present with the inner conversation that might unfold. Be curious, be the observer of your thoughts.

When you find yourself saying something negative about yourself, internally or in conversation...

Take a moment, and think 'Oh, yes, I'm about to say that about myself'. Perhaps you're about to say it out of habit, perhaps it's even a bit of a safety blanket as it means you don't really have to change. Ask yourself whether this negative thought is really very helpful. Would you say it to a friend? Come up with a positive affirmation for that moment – try one on for size instead of the boring old negative one.

I notice my thoughts with loving curiosity

Date:

Evening Reflection

Today, I am grateful for:

What went well?

What would it be good for me to hear today?

How did I meet any challenges?

Today, I am:

What do I wish to let go of?

Week 3:
Dissolving resistance

Day 18
New perspectives

It's easy to get used to looking at the world and our lives from the same angle and let that be our one truth. The problem is that human beings also happen to have a negativity bias, so we tend to look at ourselves through a lens tinted with negativity. That's why it's important not to dismiss positive affirmations if at first they feel awkward and strange (but don't they feel a little brighter and more colourful than our usual ramble of thoughts?).

Try looking up as you go for a walk. Go to the highest point nearby to give yourself a broader horizon to take in.
Look up at the stars at night.
Learn something new.

Remember to look up at the stars.

Stephen Hawking

Today I am expanding my horizons

Date:

Evening Reflection

Today, I am grateful for:

What went well?

What would it be good for me to hear today?

How did I meet any challenges?

Today, I am:

What do I wish to let go of?

Week 3:
Dissolving resistance

Day 19
Letting go of fixed outcomes

In Buddhist philosophy, expectations are considered unhelpful because they mean that we are thinking all the time about something we want to happen in the future, rather than how we are living in the present moment. Focusing on a particular outcome can create a dam in the natural flow, and even if it happens, you find yourself looking into the future once more, searching for a new outcome to strive for.

Letting go of outcomes is in no way the same as giving up on what you really want. That's the great thing about affirmations – they bring you back into relating your goals and dreams to your present experience, this moment. In whatever ways you can, how are you embodying them today?

I embrace uncertainty and all its potential

Date:

Evening Reflection

Today, I am grateful for:

What went well?

What would it be good
for me to hear today?

How did I meet any challenges?

Today, I am:

What do I wish to let go of?

Week 3: Dissolving resistance

Day 20
A meditation: Mudita

When learning that something good and wonderful has come to a friend; take a few moments, sit quietly and offer a mudita meditation by repeating either aloud or in your mind's eye:

May this bring my friend joy and happiness.

May this bring my friend more abundance.

I am happy that my friend is happy.

Repeat this a few times, then feel the energy it has created – the vibration.

If you feel your own sense of lack when you learn of the good fortune of another, remember that abundance is not a finite resource, and that we can be inspired by others. Practising what Buddhism calls 'sympathetic joy' expands our capacity for collective as well as individual happiness, connecting us all to this abundant source.

"

If I am only happy for myself, many fewer chances for happiness. If I am happy when good things happen to other people, billions more chances to be happy!

Dalai Lama

Date:

Evening Reflection

Today, I am grateful for:

What went well?

**What would it be good
for me to hear today?**

How did I meet any challenges?

Today, I am:

What do I wish to let go of?

Week 3:
Dissolving resistance

Day 21
Draw your resources

Draw yourself in the centre of the space. Now draw all the resources that you can call on – for example your resource of kindness or empathy, your resource of being really good with money, or your ability to focus and problem solve.

Everything that I need, I already have

Put it out

ting

"

You are what your deepest
desire is. As your desire is, so is
your intention. As your intention
is, so is your will. As your will is,
so is your deed. As your deed
is, so is your destiny.

Upanishads

there

Week 4:
Putting it out there

Day 22
A meditation: The bud becomes the flower

You are ever unfolding and unfurling. Life is never static, you are becoming each and every day, every moment. When you look deep inside yourself, you see your potential. You become your potential.

Imagine a rose bush, full of buds. You focus on one of the buds and under your gaze it begins to open, first the green leaves that encase the petals, and then gradually the petals themselves, coming into full bloom. The sun's rays shine on the rose, the colour is intense, nourished by the soil and water, breathing in the soft breeze.

This special rose is the rose within your own heart, coming into bloom, nourished by the sunlight of your self-compassion and made fertile by your appreciation and abundant by your unique gifts.

> ❝
> And the day came when the risk to remain tight in a bud was more painful than the risk it took to blossom.
>
> Anaïs Nin

I am growing every day

Date:

Evening Reflection

Today, I am grateful for:

What went well?

What would it be good for me to hear today?

How did I meet any challenges?

Today, I am:

What do I wish to let go of?

Week 4:
Putting it
out there

Day 23
A prompt:
Who am I now?

Write out the prompt again for
yourself and see what comes...
no editing.

Week 4:
Putting it out there

Day 24
Getting into the slipstream

Enjoy life as a flow of energy; as author and fertility expert Emma Cannon says, 'allow yourself to become part of the magical slipstream'. Bring your own gifts and energy to the world, to the Universe, with the help of your affirmations. Embrace your gifts as the medicine you have to offer. Put them out there, celebrate them, and then let them float free.

Flow with whatever is happening and let your mind be free. Stay centred by accepting whatever you are doing. This is the ultimate.

Chuang Tau

I trust the flow of life

See What Happens

Date:

Evening Reflection

I offer these gifts:

Week 4:
Putting it out there

Day 25
A practice: Movement motivation

Self-care expert Suzy Reading is both a psychologist and a yoga instructor, and she has a way of bringing the body in on the act when it comes to feeling poised and ready in an uncertain world. There is a long history of mindful movement, from rhythmic Tai Chi and Qi Gong that move and amplify energy in the body to the origins of yoga, created to help self-awareness of body and mind and connection to the Universe.

Sit comfortably in a chair with your feet flat on the floor and your back relaxed but straight, roll your shoulders a few times and gently look from side to side.

Form a steeple shape with your hands, gently spreading your fingertips wide and touching each finger and thumb together at chest height just in front of your body. Feel the pulse of your fingertips and the warmth there. This is a mudra, a hand position in yoga used to encourage clarity.

Notice the roof of your mouth creates the same shape and gently touch this with the tip of your tongue. There is a poise and peace here.

I am the architect of my life

Date:

Today, I am grateful for:

What went well?

What would it be good
for me to hear today?

How did I meet any challenges?

Today, I am:

What do I wish to let go of?

Week 4:
Putting it out there

Day 26
A practice:
Living up to my name

Dr Martin Shaw, author and
director of the Westcountry
School of Myth, offers a practice
that encourages us to embody
who we are fully and mythically
– as Martin puts it 'to profoundly
show up'. He calls this 'living up to
your name', and you simply have
to use your name as your prompt
and fill in the blanks. **Be Bold.**

—————————————— who:

—————————————— who:

—————————————— who:

—————————————— who:

—————————————— who:

—————————————— who:

Week 4:
Putting it out there

Day 27
Make a song and dance about it

Since humans first sat around a fire they have been singing and dancing, affirming life. Find a song that reflects your affirmation or make a playlist. It doesn't have to be a relentlessly positive playlist but might include places you dream of visiting or a vibe that just resonates and makes you feel energized, relaxed, peaceful or inspired.

Write out the lyrics to a favourite, affirming song:

Week 4:
Putting it out there

Day 28
Creating a daily practice

Spend a little time reflecting on the past month and what has resonated with you along the way.

Do you now have some 'go to' affirmations that help make for a good start to the day?

Can you spot negative self-talk before it starts and begin breaking those old habits of self-criticism?

Have you found it easier over time to focus a little more on your strengths and values rather than your weaknesses?

Are you more present and self-aware in your day-to-day life?

Have you begun to embrace your natural state of abundance?

Or perhaps you've found exploring affirmations a pathway to answering the biggest question of all: **Who Am I?**

What would you like to take forward with you today?